STEP TEN
Accepting Ourselves

Hazelden
Always, the pioneer

First published September, 1983

ISBN: 0-89486-178-6

Printed in the United States of America.

The following is an adaptation of one of the Twelve Steps in the program of Overeaters Anonymous. It is one person's interpretation and does not speak for the O.A. organization.

The maintenance steps

Now that you have arrived at the Tenth Step in the Overeaters Anonymous program, you are ready to maintain your recovery one day at a time for as long as you live. We use the last three Steps to stay in touch with ourselves, our Higher Power, and others in a positive, creative way. The maintenance Steps define a new way of life, one which increasingly becomes a spiritual adventure, and a physically and emotionally fulfilling experience.

As compulsive overeaters, we finally realize that the "more" that satisfies us without harm comes by way of spiritual growth. We have made progress through the first nine Steps — progress in turning our lives over to the God of our understanding, in getting rid of the mental and emotional liabilities which prevent us from knowing and doing God's will, and in cultivating assets such as courage, humility, and understanding. This is spiritual growth; the possibilities are infinite, and each day brings new challenges and opportunities. There will always be more to learn. We are rewarded with inner satisfactions that fill the emptiness we are trying to fill with excess food.

The way to keep our program alive and well, and thus maintain abstinence from compulsive overeating, is to continue growing. In this life there is no standing still. We are either moving forward or we are backsliding. The same holds true for our illness. We are either getting better or getting worse; we do not stay the same. Recovery implies continuing effort on our part, but of course we are not working alone. The daily reprieve that we are granted comes from a Higher Power and depends on our spiritual condition, as well as on the footwork we do. Step Ten helps us to stay tuned in to ourselves, our Higher Power, and other people during the ongoing process of recovery.

Sooner or later, most of us are convinced that the practice of abstinence applies to our emotional and spiritual life as well as to what we eat. Negative emotions such as anger and self-pity destroy serenity and can trigger binges. A negative spiritual state — for instance, giving way to pride, greed, doubt, or dishonesty — is equally damaging. If we lose contact with our Higher Power and let our emotions run riot, we will probably do all sorts of harm to ourselves and those around us, and we will be in danger of slipping back into compulsive overeating. To avoid backsliding, we need to keep building up assets like honesty, courage, faith, responsibility, understanding, and love of others.

Maintaining our program is literally a life and death choice. O.A. offers a way of controlling a progressive illness, which if not treated can destroy its victims. The Twelve Steps have proved successful in arresting the illness. It has also been proven that one can stop practicing the Steps, drop out of the program, and commit slow suicide (sometimes not so slow).

Experience indicates that once we become compulsive overeaters our potential for abusing food is always present. It is too easy to fall back into old habits. We are offered a new life of recovery, but this gift depends on daily attention to our emotional and spiritual development. No one else is going to do it for us. If we want the benefits promised by the program, we have to do our part. There is no graduation ceremony, but there is gratifying progress as we go to meetings, work the Steps, and stay in touch with a Higher Power.

What's going on

Step Ten suggests that we continue taking personal inventory and promptly admit our mistakes. This Step is a tool that helps us to be straight about what's really happening in our lives and to make immediate amends when we see that we are wrong. Step Ten is crucial to the continued improvement of interpersonal relationships, which in turn makes it easier to abstain from compulsive overeating. We maintain our willingness to admit where we are at fault in a conflict, and we are also willing to forgive when someone else has made a mistake. We do not have to fall back on the unsatisfactory consolation of excessive eating.

How do you know when to take an inventory? Many of us find it helpful to practice the Tenth Step at the end of each day, going over our actions and attitudes during that particular twenty-four hour period — a type of daily self-examination. Was our abstinence cleaner? Did we refrain from criticizing the people we live with? Did we make a useful contribution to someone else's day? We review where we made progress with the program and where we got off the track, considering how to repair any damage we may have done and how to avoid the same mistakes tomorrow. We congratulate ourselves for positive actions and feelings (as well as for temptations overcome), and we reaffirm our relationship with a Higher Power.

At any hour of the day, if we are getting upset or feel that our abstinence is being threatened, it is time to stop and take a quick inventory. In the *Twelve Steps and Twelve Traditions,* this part of Step Ten is called a spot-check. If we are angry with a co-worker and feel our serenity slipping, we don't have to wait until we hit the ceiling or our colleague before we stop to think. We are not responsible for what someone else does, but we are responsible for our reactions. We have a choice as to how we will act in a given situation. If we're upset, that's our problem and we need to deal with it. For instance, if we see that our anger is coming out of false pride, we can choose to let go of it. A spot-check inventory reveals how our attitude and response to events beyond our control, such as someone else's words or actions, can strengthen rather than weaken our recovery.

Then there are the circumstances which call for a major housecleaning at least once a year. Have new problems accumulated since we took our Fourth Step? Are the same old problems coming back? If for a period of time we have been feeling confused and out of touch with ourselves, those around us, or our Higher Power, we may need to actually sit down and write out another inventory for review with our sponsor or someone else. We might plan for an annual review, similar to yearly physical examination, as a preventive measure.

However we decide to use Step Ten, we have a program which offers a plan of action when something is wrong. This is one of the reasons we can be grateful that we are recovering compulsive overeaters. We have a built-in barometer that tells us when we're off base. When we begin to have trouble with food, emotions, other people, or all of them together, we can be sure that we have wandered away from the program and from our Higher Power. We can be grateful that by way of the illness we have found a new guide for living. Because of our weakness, we have turned to a Power greater than ourselves, a source of strength which we otherwise might not have experienced.

Do you find yourself waking up in the clutches of some

dreadful anxiety that sets your mind going in circles? Do you go through too many days with a cloud of self-pity hanging over your head? Are you caught in a relationship that you know is harmful?

Our tendency is to blame circumstances and other people for whatever is wrong in our lives. As the program keeps reminding us, this is counterproductive. We are powerless over other people and events. What we can do is take our inventory, see where our own liabilities are getting in the way of our program, and admit our part in whatever conflict is destroying our serenity.

This may happen many times a day. How often do you try to control the people around you, dictating their actions and then getting mad when they do not do what you think they should? The sooner you realize what you are doing, apologize, and back off, the sooner your energy will be free for constructive action. Rather than allowing a conflict to grow, we can do something about it immediately if we recognize our part in it and turn the angry feelings over to a Higher Power. Stop and think before you say or do something you will later regret. Let go of self-will. Let the other person be right. Let your Higher Power determine the outcome of events, even such simple ones as what will happen if your friend doesn't listen to your directions and gets lost.

As compulsive overeaters, we have all used food to mask our feelings. "Oh no, nothing is wrong," you said to yourself and everyone else, in spite of the fact that you were filled with resentment because someone let you down. And then you ate. None of us has to do that anymore. We have a program, and we have tools. We can admit, especially to ourselves, that there is a problem, and we can proceed to find out what it is and what can be done about it. (Did you feel let down because your expectations were unrealistic?) Remember, in any given situation we are only responsible for taking our own personal inventory.

Name them, claim them, dump them

The advantage of taking inventory when we are awash with negative emotions is that we are able to recognize the feelings, admit that we own and are responsible for them, and then let them go. We do not have to hang on to painful emotions, or use an excuse to overeat; we can choose to turn them over — again and again. "Let go and let God."

Writing is one of the valuable tools of the O.A. program. When you are not sure just what it is that is troubling you, take out paper and pencil and start putting down in black and white what you are feeling. Instead of going into a "blue funk," snapping at your best friend, and heading for the nearest fast-food restaurant, write! Write until your pencil begins to reveal what is really going on inside your head.

This stream-of-consciousness inventory can be for our eyes only. If we know before we start what is bothering us, writing can be a way of getting rid of it. The very act of putting our feelings into words on paper helps to dissipate the anger, fear, resentment, or self-pity. When we look at what we have written, we may see our previously overwhelming emotional reaction shrink into manageability. Then we can tear up the paper instead of hurling invectives at the person we live with, or stuffing ourselves with food.

Sometimes we may want to go over what we have written with another person. Should I look for a new job? Ask for a raise? From Fifth Step experience, we know that sharing our hurts, fears, guilts, and anxieties liberates us from having to carry them around indefinitely. In the past we attempted to be independent and manage our own lives and our own problems, but that didn't work. Hopefully we have now learned enough humility through these Steps so that we can go to a trusted friend or sponsor and get help when we need it. Often the other person can assist simply by being a sounding board. Defining a problem out loud makes it more manageable than continuing to go around and around the same old solitary mental track. Someone else can often hear what we are saying behind and underneath our actual words; their perception puts the situation into a new light.

Regularly looking inward to identify the reason we're upset works wonders with relationships. If we see that our desire to be in control has triggered a fight with our spouse, we can admit it, say we're sorry, and let go. When the insight occurs sooner rather than later, much emotional pain can be avoided. Though we can probably *name* our partner's character defects more easily than our own, ours are the only ones we are able to claim and dump.

Step Ten gives us a way to take our emotional and spiritual temperature and apply treatment when needed. Once we identify and admit where we have been wrong, we can choose to let go of those mistakes and any regrets attached to them. If we are in contact with a Higher Power, we are living *now,* not in the past. We cannot change what has happened. It is over and done with. To regret what we cannot change is to keep ourselves bound to the past instead of alive to God's will for our lives here and now, in the present. Self-examination helps us to learn from past mistakes, but we do not need to dwell on them. We were wrong. We see that now. We have said that we are sorry. Since we believe that our Higher Power forgives us, we can forgive ourselves and move on, preferably out of the kitchen.

Forgiveness is a prerequisite to letting go of negative feelings —

to forgive others and ourselves, over and over again. We do not need to wallow in guilt over mistakes. It has been pointed out that excess guilt can be an inverse form of pride; we expect ourselves to be perfect. By promptly admitting where we were wrong, we can avoid self-imposed guilt trips. We will never be perfect, but we are learning and making progress.

New possibilities

"We can try to stop making unreasonable demands upon those we love. We can show kindness where we had shown none. With those we dislike we can begin to practice justice and courtesy, perhaps going out of our way to understand and help them."*

Gradually, we are moving off center stage. When we discover that clinging to self-will defeats us every time, we can abandon our attempts to satisfy the great "I want." Just as abstinence teaches us to eat what we need, so the Steps of the O.A. program teach the art of give and take. As we become more committed to knowing and doing God's will, it is easier to think about the needs and feelings of other people. Honestly trying to do what a Higher Power wants us to do, we can be more tolerant, more fair, and more generous, even with individuals we don't particularly like. The pay-off is that we end up feeling better ourselves.

Through this program, we are learning how to live comfortably without escaping into excess food. For a time, this may make us more vulnerable to emotional ups and downs. Along with

*Twelve Steps and Twelve Traditions, published by A.A. World Services, New York, NY, p. 93. Available through Hazelden Educational Materials.

being dependent on food to cushion the hard knocks of living, we may also have been overly dependent on other people, expecting them to jump when we pulled the strings and cater to our whims. Gradually, we are relinquishing our frustrating attempts to control and manipulate.

Although moving off center stage means that we are considerably easier to live with, we are certainly not going to turn into saints. The difference is that now we are better able to catch ourselves when we are winding up for conflict and more willing to say, "Excuse me. I didn't mean to step on you. I don't expect you to read my mind and to satisfy my every wish. Let's just agree to be human together. When something hurts, we can say 'ouch' without starting the Third World War."

When we don't take ourselves too seriously, and when we don't always have to be right and in control, conflicts abate. In Step Three, when we turned our will and our life over to the God of our understanding, we agreed that He would run the show, and we are trying to act according to His direction. This means being willing to let go of whatever separates us from our Higher Power — fear, anger, pride, resentment — because as recovering compulsive overeaters, we cannot afford these negative feelings, no matter how convinced we are that they are justified. We know from sad experience that negative emotions, justified or not, will undermine our recovery.

With spiritual growth comes greater tolerance of the weaknesses of other people. Now that we know we are being cared for by a Higher Power, we do not have to hang on to impossibly high expectations of our fellow human beings. They are struggling, too, and like us are doing the best they can. Our security and self-esteem no longer depend on the illusion of having perfect friends, an ideal partner, exemplary children, or all-wise parents.

When we were overeating, most of us did not like ourselves or anyone else. Through abstinence and the Twelve Steps, we discover, often slowly, that the source of friction between ourselves and others is within us. When we are in harmony internally, it is possible to be in harmony with those around us as well. It is possible to let go of unreasonable demands. When we can accept and begin to like ourselves, we can be more generous with everyone else. We discover that being part of the chorus can be a lot more enjoyable than fighting to stay on center stage.

Tenth-stepping with love

"This is a good place to remember that inventory-taking is not always done in red ink. It's a poor day indeed when we haven't done *something* right. As a matter of fact, the waking hours are usually well-filled with things that are constructive. Good intentions, good thoughts, and good acts are there for us to see. Even when we have tried hard and failed, we may chalk that up as one of the greatest credits of all."*

What have we done right today? Did we take a few moments to talk to someone who seemed to need cheering up? Did we put the top back on the toothpaste tube without criticizing the person who left it off? Did we try again to have an abstinent day?

Important as it is, abstinence alone does not fill our lives. Abstinence frees us from compulsive overeating so that we can love ourselves and other people and turn our energies toward productive, enjoyable activities. If we are abstaining out of a sense of "ought," or in order to be "good," or so that we can wear a size eight, we will probably run out of steam before very long.

---

*Ibid., p. 93.

Tenth-stepping with love means that we forgive ourselves when certain actions do not measure up to the standards we have set. We come home tired and uptight over a problem at the office. We make mincemeat out of nine-year-old Billy who has left his bicycle in the middle of the driveway for the eighty-seventh time, eat four doughnuts, and kick the dog. Not so good.

When the dust settles and we are back on the track, after having telephoned a friend in the program, read some O.A. literature, or simply spent several minutes quietly getting in touch with our Higher Power, the first thing we do is make peace with Billy. Then we forgive ourselves for breaking our abstinence and being a "rotten parent." (And we pet the dog.) Then we think about how we can avoid some of the stress and fatigue that sabotages our recovery. Perhaps we even glimpse how a change in our attitude could improve things at the office.

Tenth-stepping with love means that we refrain from playing games with other people's feelings. If we have landed in a relationship where we are using another person in a selfish, dependent way, but are unwilling to make a genuine commitment, Step Ten says we need to admit that to ourselves and to the other person. Honesty may not be easy, but not being honest is harder in the long run. Besides, when we are being straight with ourselves and others, we do not need to overeat.

Tenth-stepping with love means that we look for ways to fill our lives with positive experiences. As we take inventory in the O.A. program we measure our wealth not by what we have in stock, but by what we have given away. We look for opportunities to be of service to other people. We are willing to try and fail, and try again. We care. We are alive. We are learning — one day at a time.